UNDERSTANDING
The Dynamics of Multiplication

BARUCH
Publishing

UNDERSTANDING the Dynamics of Multiplication

God's Order and System for Growing and Discipling His Church for His Purpose

Dr. John A. Tetsola

Understanding the Dynamics of Multiplication
God's Order and System for Growing and Discipling His Church for His Purpose

Copyright ©2023 by Dr. John A. Tetsola First Printing. Printed and bound in the United States of America. All rights reserved. No part of this book may be reproduced in any form or by any means, including information storage and retrieval systems, without written permission from the publisher, except by a reviewer, who may quote brief passages in a review. Published by Baruch Publishing, P.O. Box 743, Bronx, NY 10462.

ISBN 978-1-948033-57-2

Scripture quotations marked (KJV) are takenfrom the King James Version of the Bible.

Scripture quotations marked (AMPC) are taken from the Amplified Bible, Classic Edition. Copyright © 1954, 1958, 1962, 1964, 1965, 1987 by The Lockman Foundation.

Scripture quotations marked (NIV) are taken from The New International Version Holy Bible, New International Version®, NIV® Copyright ©1973, 1978, 1984, 2011 by Biblica, Inc.® Used by permission. All rights reserved worldwide.

Note: In some Scripture quotations, italics have been added by the author for emphasis only.

TABLE OF CONTENTS

Chapter One
Spiritual Addition Versus
Spiritual Multiplication...1

Chapter Two
The Three Essentials of Kingdom
Multiplication..13

Chapter Three
The Four Capacities Needed for
Multiplication..19

Chapter Four
The Three Common Mistakes in Spiritual
Multiplication..25

CHAPTER ONE

Spiritual Addition Versus Spiritual Multiplication

Spiritual addition in ministry is when someone wins other people to Christ, but does not disciple, train, and deepen those converts to go out and do likewise. While we will review the biblical basis for spiritual multiplication, for now let it suffice to state that in Matthew 28:18-20, we are commanded to go and make disciples, not simply converts.

> Jesus approached and, breaking the silence, said to them, All authority (all power of rule) in heaven and on earth has been given to Me.
>
> Go then and make disciples of all the nations, baptizing them into the name of the Father and of the Son and of the Holy Spirit,
>
> Teaching them to observe everything that I have commanded you, and behold, I am with you all the days (perpetually, uniformly, and on every occasion), to the [very] close and consummation of the age. Amen (so let it be).
>
> *Matthew 28:18-20 AMPC*

If you led a thousand people to Christ every year for 36 years (taking each one through basic follow up), how many people would you have reached with the gospel? Answer: 36,000. However, if you led three people to Christ, discipled them, and trained each one to reach three other people, and everyone that was discipled in turn reached three other people each year, then when we multiply the process out over 36 years the number of disciples becomes 1,048,576. That's exponential growth. That's spiritual multiplication. This seems to be what the Lord had in mind in the Great Commission, as it makes the completion of the task feasible as it's doubtful that Jesus expected His disciples to keep up a case load of one thousand disciples a year.

The Biblical Precedent for Spiritual Multiplication

> Him we preach and proclaim, warning and admonishing everyone and instructing everyone in all wisdom ([a]comprehensive insight into the ways and purposes of God), that we may present every person mature (full-grown, fully initiated, complete, and perfect) in Christ (the Anointed One).
>
> *Colossians 1:28 AMPC*

We have already alluded to the precedence of the Great Commission in the book of Matthew, but there is other biblical support for this model. What follows is a brief survey.Colossians 1:28 states that every man is complete in Christ. The goal is not conversion but completion, or as Matthew 28:19 states it, "teaching them to observe all that I have commanded you." Not just some of what Jesus had commanded, but all. In Ephesians, we read:

> His intention was the perfecting and the full equipping of the saints (His consecrated people), [that they should do] the work of ministering toward building up Christ's body (the church),

Spiritual Addition Versus Spiritual Multiplication

[That it might develop] until we all attain oneness in the faith and in the comprehension of the [full and accurate] knowledge of the Son of God, that [we might arrive] at really mature manhood (the completeness of personality which is nothing less than the standard height of Christ's own perfection), the measure of the stature of the fullness of the Christ and the completeness found in Him.

So then, we may no longer be children, tossed [like ships] to and fro between chance gusts of teaching and wavering with every changing wind of doctrine, [the prey of] the cunning and cleverness of unscrupulous men, [gamblers engaged] in every shifting form of trickery in inventing errors to mislead.

Rather, let our lives lovingly express truth [in all things, speaking truly, dealing truly, living truly]. Enfolded in love, let us grow up in every way and in all things into Him Who is the Head, [even] Christ (the Messiah, the Anointed One).

For because of Him the whole body (the church, in all its various parts), closely joined and firmly knit together by the joints and ligaments with which it is supplied, when each part [with power adapted to its need] is working properly [in all its functions], grows to full maturity, building itself up in love.

Ephesians 4:12-16 AMPC

These passages underscore that it is God's will that all who come to faith should grow into maturity in Christ and become full in the true knowledge of Him, fulfilling God's desire for their character and their ministry. In verse 12, it says that the saints are to be equipped "for the work of service, to the building up of the body of Christ." We are to do this "until we all (there is that word again!) attain to the unity of the faith." Again, mere conversion is not what God prescribes.

> And the [instructions] which you have heard from me along with many witnesses, transmit and entrust [as a deposit] to reliable and faithful men who will be competent and qualified to teach others also.
>
> *2 Timothy 2:2 AMPC*

The emphasis in this verse is on multiplication. Notice the connection between the teacher, his students, and his students' students. There is a long-range view to discipleship versus a terminal one. Teaching does not simply start with a teacher and end with his students. It is to go on to the students' students, their students and so on. The idea of one generation teaching the next is explicit here in the text. It supports the view of spiritual multiplication as opposed to mere spiritual addition.

> For because of Him the whole body (the church, in all its various parts), closely joined and firmly knit together by the joints and ligaments with which it is supplied, when each part [with power adapted to its need] is working properly [in all its functions], grows to full maturity, building itself up in love.
>
> *Ephesians 4:16 AMPC*

This idea of connection is explicit in this text. Look at the language the Holy Spirit has apostle Paul employ: "the whole body, being fitted and held together by that which every joint supplies." This runs counter to the more modern, Western view of rugged individualism wherein we have lone rangers doing ministry while others are on the sidelines watching. A ministry of addition leads to this kind of mentality. If one person is doing all the evangelism, or all the discipleship, and there isn't any plan for delegation, we're swimming against the tide of the New Testament. God intends there to be spiritual multiplication in our ministries.

Old Testament Precedent

There is also an emphasis upon spiritual multiplication in the Old Testament. Look at Exodus 18. In this passage, Jethro confronts Moses for trying to lead Israel single-handedly, teaching the Law and implementing its particulars on his own.

- *First, Jethro displays his concerns for Moses:*

    When Moses' father-in-law saw all that he was doing for the people, he said, What is this that you do for the people? Why do you sit alone, and all the people stand around you from morning till evening?

    You will surely wear out both yourself and this people with you, for the thing is too heavy for you; you are not able to perform it all by yourself.

    Exodus 18:14, 18 AMPC

The indictment of "doing it alone" has a sting to it, and it's obvious that Moses ought to delegate. But, before we get to the solution, notice it says not only that Moses the leader will be worn out if he doesn't change his ways, but, also, the "people who are with [him]." What does this mean? Can we surmise that it is wearisome to those around us when we don't include them in the work of God's kingdom? Is it because a leader is hoarding the task and has marginalized those around him? This makes for some very interesting conjecture.

- *Second, Jethro outlines his solution to Moses:*

    Listen now to [me]; I will counsel you, and God will be with you. You shall represent the people before God, bringing their cases and causes to Him,

> Teaching them the decrees and laws, showing them the way they must walk and the work they must do.
>
> Moreover, you shall choose able men from all the people—God-fearing men of truth who hate unjust gain—and place them over thousands, hundreds, fifties, and tens, to be their rulers.
>
> And let them judge the people at all times; every great matter they shall bring to you, but every small matter they shall judge. So it will be easier for you, and they will bear the burden with you.
>
> If you will do this, and God so commands you, you will be able to endure [the strain], and all these people also will go to their [tents] in peace.
>
> Exodus 18:19-23 AMPC

Again, we see delegation and multiplication—leaders who in turn teach leaders, who in turn teach leaders, and so on. This strongly supports the notion that spiritual multiplication is biblically prescribed for us as the way in which God intends His kingdom to function. This is something we see in both the Old and New Testaments.

Tips for Developing and Excelling in Spiritual Multiplication

We first looked at a comparison between spiritual addition and spiritual multiplication. We then briefly explored the biblical precedence for spiritual multiplication. Now, we want to examine some ways that we can excel in the task of spiritual multiplication. While there are many ways to go about this, I will give you my top eight suggestions.

- Tip 1—Leaders start and stay focused with the end in mind.

Effectiveness is linked to viewing a worthy goal before one begins working on the task. Certainly, spiritual multiplication is a worthy goal. When a leader works toward that end, a view of it must be in her mind at all times as she pursues it. So, we start by focusing upon the end in mind: spiritual multiplication. We are not simply thinking of our discipleship, or even their disciples, but a step further. We communicate with the expectation that what we teach will be handed down a line or chain of disciples. This informs what and how we disciple.

- Tip 2—Leaders seek to be servants.

One of the more significant paradigms a leader needs to embrace is the concept of servanthood, not only to be obedient to the Lord, but to be effective in spiritual multiplication. Leaders need to see that their disciples have been entrusted to them. We are to help them live fruitful lives, and serve them toward this end, never selfishly seeking the expanse of our own ministry.

- TIP 3—Leaders think deeply about the content they are exposing to their disciples.

There are whole libraries on the subject of spiritual growth and multiplication. It would be presumptuous to think that a few paragraphs could do justice to this topic. So, let's look at the outline found in Ephesians:

> And His gifts were [varied; He Himself appointed and gave men to us] some to be apostles (special messengers), some prophets (inspired preachers and expounders), some evangelists (preachers of the Gospel, traveling missionaries), some pastors (shepherds of His flock) and teachers.
>
> His intention was the perfecting and the full equipping of the saints (His consecrated people),

[that they should do] the work of ministering toward building up Christ's body (the church),

[That it might develop] until we all attain oneness in the faith and in the comprehension of the [full and accurate] knowledge of the Son of God, that [we might arrive] at really mature manhood (the completeness of personality which is nothing less than the standard height of Christ's own perfection), the measure of the stature of the fullness of the Christ and the completeness found in Him.

So then, we may no longer be children, tossed [like ships] to and fro between chance gusts of teaching and wavering with every changing wind of doctrine, [the prey of] the cunning and cleverness of unscrupulous men, [gamblers engaged] in every shifting form of trickery in inventing errors to mislead.

Rather, let our lives lovingly express truth [in all things, speaking truly, dealing truly, living truly]. Enfolded in love, let us grow up in every way and in all things into Him Who is the Head, [even] Christ (the Messiah, the Anointed One).

For because of Him the whole body (the church, in all its various parts), closely joined and firmly knit together by the joints and ligaments with which it is supplied, when each part [with power adapted to its need] is working properly [in all its functions], grows to full maturity, building itself up in love.

Ephesians 4:11-16 AMPC

The "menu" has five major headings:

- Training: "Equipping the saints" (v. 12).

- Doctrine: "Unity of the faith, knowledge of the Son of God" (v. 13).

- Character: "Mature man, the fullness of Christ" (v. 13).

- Team Effectiveness Skills: Relational effectiveness, communication skills, team building skills, personality and temperament awareness. "Speaking the truth in love, fitted and held together by that which every joint supplies" (vv. 15-16).

- Unique Contribution: "The proper working of each individual part" (v. 16).

Select material or experiences that balance the above to ensure a balance of multiplication and growth in your disciples.

- Tip 4—Leaders know content isn't the only focus.

Leaders know that if they only focus on the content of what is being imparted (teaching, experiences, training, etc.), the process of spiritual multiplication will abort or be immature. So much of discipleship and spiritual multiplication is dependent upon relationships. There needs to be an atmosphere of grace, time to just hang out together, and opportunities for the leader to model the Christian life—not just talk about it.

- TIP 5—Leaders continue in evangelism.

In discipleship, it is easy to let evangelism slide into the background. But it must remain front and center, because this is where the future disciples are going to come from. This is also the whole point of the Great Commission—"go and make disciples." Sometimes, in the effort to make disciples, unconsciously, evangelism takes a secondary role instead of discipling in the context of evangelism.

Content apart from the practice of the ministry becomes seminary, not discipleship.

- TIP 6—Leaders rely on praying to a sovereign God.

Leaders instinctively know that given God's sovereign rule and reign, nothing will happen apart from Him (John 15:5). So, they are vigilant in prayer, in their planning, their teaching, their evangelism, and their selection of disciples. God is the author of it all and unless the Lord builds the multiplication chain, they labor in vain who build it (a paraphrase of Psalm 127:1).

- TIP 7—Leaders pay heed to the importance of selection.

> And the [instructions] which you have heard from me along with many witnesses, transmit and entrust [as a deposit] to reliable and faithful men who will be competent and qualified to teach others also.
>
> *2 Timothy 2:2 AMPC*

Let's look at 2 Timothy 2:2 as we consider selection (the process of deciding who to invest your life into). When Paul uses the expression "qualified to teach others also," it is implying that we are to make judgments as to whether or not a potential disciple is indeed "able to teach." In other words, is the potential disciple someone who not only has the intellectual capability but the character as well? A helpful acrostic is S.T.A.F., which stands for Social, Teachable, Available, and Faithful. In the mode of selection, the leader ought to be looking for disciples who are:

- Able to relate well enough for people to follow.

- Willing to learn.

- Free enough from scheduling demands (e.g. school work, job, family).

- TIP 8—Leaders remember to encourage yourselves

Taking on the colossal task of spiritual multiplication brings with it challenges from within and without. There is criticism, attacks of the enemy, and loads of self-doubt. So being planted in rich, vital fellowship with other leaders is critical for encouragement.

CHAPTER TWO

The Three Essentials Of Kingdom Multiplication

> But you shall receive power (ability, efficiency, and might) when the Holy Spirit has come upon you, and you shall be My witnesses in Jerusalem and all Judea and Samaria and to the ends (the very bounds) of the earth.
>
> *Acts 1:8 AMPC*

The plan for kingdom multiplication begins with a mission." This quote from modern management pioneer Peter Drucker gives us a good indicator of how important it is to understand our mission or why the church exists. The words in Jesus' Great Commission gives us our mission: biblical disciple-making. Any other core mission will take us off track, failing to lead to healthy multiplication and movements of His witnesses (the commandment Jesus gives us in Acts 1:8). Simply put, the core of any multiplication movement is disciple-making. The general or common calling shared by all Christians, everywhere, throughout all time, is to follow Jesus' command that we are disciples who make disciples wherever we are!

#1
Disciple Making: The First Dimension

Assuming you embrace this core purpose, the most important question to ask then is, "What type of disciples are we making?" Are you producing biblical disciples who make disciples that plant churches? Or are you largely making cultural Christians that feed your church's numerical growth, but don't make disciples who multiply? I'm convinced that if we want to understand why we aren't seeing movements of exponential multiplication, we should start by looking at the quality of our disciple-making.

Are you producing biblical disciples who make disciples that plant churches that plant churches? We can look at disciple-making through the lens of adding disciples (making converts) and reproducing (making disciples). The pathways for adding disciples—connecting with people, introducing them to Jesus, and bringing them to a point of accepting Him as Lord—are the entry points to making biblical disciples. We add people one follower at a time. Infants in the faith spiritually mature and then reproduce themselves, repeating the cycle.

By making biblical disciples, we become more effective at carrying the fullness of Jesus into every corner of our communities, ultimately sending disciples to go and multiply new churches that create even greater capacity for healthy Kingdom growth. Disciples who make disciples the way Jesus did are the fuel of multiplication movements.

#2
Building Disciple Making Capacity: The Second Dimension

As critical as disciple making is to multiplication, on its own it does not guarantee multiplication. We also need to build the infrastructure or capacity necessary to expand and support our disciple-making context. The key question is, "What type of capacity are we building?"

Think about how Jesus spent three years building the core capacity for the greatest movement in history. By embedding the gospel DNA for disciple making into twelve followers surrendered to His Lordship, He built capacity. Those twelve leaders passed along the genetic code to others who did the same for others on their path. I love the fact that the right capacity for the right motives built into a small band of believers can change the world. The institutional part of church, including its infrastructure, processes and resources, is vital to multiplying and sustaining your church's growth via disciple making.

Have you ever thought that every believer in your church has the capacity for a multiplication movement? Do you grasp that profound truth? In His wisdom, God gave us the Church—in part because we are designed to function like a family, and also to provide us with a platform of capacity for:

1. Increasing our effectiveness in disciple making, and

2. Scaling or multiplying our efforts at disciple making (beyond what unaffiliated, lone ranger disciples can do when they're separated from biblical fellowship).

#3
Mobilizing Disciples to Make Disciples: The Third Dimension

As a leader, your role is to simultaneously manage the tensions in these first two dimensions of multiplication: disciple making and building capacity. But these two key dimensions are not enough to fulfill Jesus' command to "go." We must also mobilize disciples to carry the fullness of Jesus into every corner of society as they make disciples. But mobilization gives us two simultaneous tensions to manage. Scripture calls us to "live in common" as a family of believers via the church community—much like the Acts 2 church. Look at the collective "they" statements we find in Acts 2:

- They met daily.

- They broke bread together.

- They had everything in common.

- They sold property and possessions to give to those in need.

At the same time, we're called to "live deployed" as missionaries in our unique corners of society. We each have a mission field of influence and a specific gifting. This dual command often creates a tension in our churches. Think about an aircraft carrier. Its mission is to send air power to places the carrier can't go. To carry out that mission, five thousand men and women work, eat, and do life together. Out of that five thousand, only one hundred twenty fly the planes. In the same way, the average church has an army of volunteers living in common to support the work of the paid, full-time professional pastors (the pilots).

This is not the way Jesus intended the Church to function. We are each to live in common, doing whatever we need to do to support the family, while simultaneously going into our unique corners of society. When we don't use our unique calling and gifts to go, we negatively impact Jesus' mission for His Church. When we do find ways to lead our churches so that we're simultaneously living in common and living deployed, we mobilize biblical disciples to go and be Kingdom multipliers!

CHAPTER THREE

The Four Capacities Needed For Multiplication

Congregations that are ready to launch successful new initiatives typically possess four strands of congregational DNA—spiritual intensity, missional alignment, dynamic relationships, and cultural openness. Measuring and strengthening these four capacities can prepare the church to leap from maintenance multiplication.

Multiplication can mean many different things for a church. Sometimes new small groups, new worship communities, new hubs of activity, new people groups, new age-level ministries, new outreach initiatives, the proliferation of new ministry teams, new campuses, even new congregations that your church might help plant.

Multiplication also means the same things in every church. Leaders helping to recruit, form, and release new leaders. People letting go of the status quo in order to expand the church's reach and to share Christ with others. Thinking about the mission beyond simply caring for folks already inside. And carefully evaluating everything you do in light of your stated purpose. Congregations that are ready to create new places and launch successful new ministry initiatives typically possess four strands of congregational DNA that mark their ability to multiply leaders, ministries, worship, and even launch new faith communities.

■ *Spiritual intensity*

Is your congregation driven by its passion for Christ? All of the great church movements worldwide are intense spiritually, marked by a deep love for God and a surrendering to what God is seeking to do through human beings. Understanding the degree to which a spiritual fire burns within the hearts and souls of those leading and participating in the life of the church is critical. Characteristics of congregations with strong spiritual intensity include:

- Many people have an expectation of encountering the living Christ personally and/or in the congregation.

- Practicing spiritual disciplines (prayer, Bible study, fasting, Christian works, and so on) is an important part of life together.

- People are willing to take risks as an expression of their faith and trust in God.

- Leaders—paid and unpaid—demonstrate spiritual vitality.

- *Missional alignment*

Does your activity flow from your stated values? The degree to which a church consistently prioritizes investment of its resources (time, talent, treasure) according to a biblical vision and mission indicates readiness in this dimension. It is critical that your church's plans, major initiatives, and pruning of ministry stem clearly from a biblical vision/mission and drive for fruitfulness instead of from habit. Characteristics of churches with strong missional alignment include:

- A clear understanding of their mandate to reach new people.

- Alignment to a clear direction.

- Good strategic thinking that is a regular part of leadership conversations.

- The ability to make decisions about resources based on priority as opposed to pleasing people or maintaining the status quo. Preference is the enemy of obedience.

- A shared sense of competency about the church's ability to start new ministries.

- *Dynamic relationships*

How dynamic and healthy are your relationships with those inside and outside your church? Good habits and skills for leading new persons into a deeper relationship with God through Christ is vital. Healthy congregations work as a system to accomplish this. Your relationships with others directly impact the strength of your evangelism muscle. Characteristics of congregations with healthy, dynamic relationships include:

- The practice of strong welcoming behaviors—more than a program but a way of being with newcomers.

- A strong track record of bringing people from the outside into participation in the community of faith.

- Positive experiences partnering with other leaders and groups.

- A culture of healthy teamwork and leader development—including healthy conflict management skills.

■ *Cultural openness*

Does your congregation exhibit a capacity for embracing people from diverse cultures? Since the first century, effective churches have been reaching across cultural boundaries to share the Christian good news with diverse people who begin with different experiences, perspectives, and stories. Churches that exhibit fortress behaviors or who spend excessive time mourning social change often have difficulty sharing life with new kinds of people. Characteristics of congregations with strong cultural openness include:

- A collection of attitudes and behaviors that support receptivity to folks who aren't like them.

- A good ability to form meaningful community with people who puzzle and/or offend you in certain respects.

- A perception that diversity in church is a good thing.

- Energy for working with different kinds of people.

- Willingness and ability to share power with new people.

- Valuable experiences that help them reach people in their neighborhood that aren't like them.

Are you interested in changing the trajectory of your church from maintenance to gospel movement? From stagnation toward life, renewal and a future that is befitting the Christian gospel. Measuring and strengthening these four strands of multiplication DNA in your faith community can prepare your church to make the leap from church maintenance to gospel movement.

CHAPTER FOUR

The Three Common Mistakes In Spiritual Multiplication

> And other seed [of the same kind] fell into good (well-adapted) soil and brought forth grain, growing up and increasing, and yielded up to thirty times as much, and sixty times as much, and even a hundred times as much as had been sown.
>
> *Mark 4:8 AMPC*

All of my life I remeber the multiplication tables. We were tested with those flash cards. But, what about a different kind of multiplication. The overwhelming potential for spiritual multiplication through healthy discipleship haunts me. It also drives me. That is one of the reasons I do ministry. Even a small ministry that multiplies disciples can impact thousands of people in just a few years.

- *Losing your focus on multiplication as the goal*

Multiplication doesn't happen by accident. It must be intentionally pursued. Let me plead with you not to be guilty of practicing what I call "dead-end discipleship." Dead-end discipleship is when Christians meet with Christians to make them more Christian but don't ever break out of Christian subculture to engage lost people.

Discipleship without evangelism is not discipleship. It's actually recycle-ship. Too often what passes as spiritual multiplication is nothing more than reorganizing Christians. There are no shortcuts to experiencing true spiritual multiplication. We need disciples who have the faith, courage and spiritual maturity to "labor" among lost people until God saves someone. Here are some practical things we do in order to ensure that our discipleship is focused on reproducing:

1. At the beginning of every discipling relationship, start praying together for the conversion of your lost friends and family. Keep expanding this prayer list.

2. Encourage disciples to choose a "pocket of people" with whom to build relationships and begin broadly sharing the gospel as opportunities arise.

3. Take them with you when you have gospel appointments with new people who visit your ministry. If someone comes to Christ you could have your disciple do the follow-up with the person. It's important that they gain experience in practical ministry.

4. Make sure that all you do is simple to reproduce. You want them to say, "That's it? Even I could do that!"

5. As you are training people in a particular spiritual discipline or essential concept, make sure to infuse the vision for reproduction into the process. I love the phrase, "When you are discipling someone this is how you could explain this concept."

6. Pray daily and specifically that God would grow your disciples into laborers and that He would provide them with someone to disciple soon. Pray together for this during your meetings.

7. Provide coaching and training once they start discipling others. Spend time each meeting discussing how it is going with those they are discipling and what it will take for that person to begin discipling others.

Multiplication takes time. Don't stress if you are not seeing multiplication happen overnight. Focus on quality, and God may provide the quantity at the proper time. It's not how many men, but what kind of men.

- *Giving up on people too soon*

It's so easy to lose patience with people when they are flaky or seem unmotivated. The older I get, the more jaded I am tempted to become. But then I realize how many of our core leaders were once flaky freshman, and I am encouraged. There is actually a difference between follow-up and discipleship training. When following-up with a new believer, you don't practice the principle of selection. Pursue a new believer until they tell you to stop. They are babies who need milk.

> Like newborn babies you should crave (thirst for, earnestly desire) the pure (unadulterated) spiritual milk, that by it you may be nurtured and grow unto [completed] salvation,
>
> *1 Peter 2:2 AMPC*

We have to remember that new believers are babies spiritually. We can't be selective with them too soon.

> But we behaved gently when we were among you, like a devoted mother nursing and cherishing her own children.
>
> So, being thus tenderly and affectionately desirous of you, we continued to share with you not only God's good news (the Gospel) but also our own lives as well, for you had become so very dear to us.
>
> *1 Thessalonians 2:7-8 AMPC*

People are not naturally "F.A.T." Faithful. Available. Teachable. However, they can be trained in these things. Just because someone is sending you mixed signals about how interested they are doesn't mean God is not working in their life. Keep praying for them, loving them and seeking to get them connected.

> Be gentle and forbearing with one another and, if one has a difference (a grievance or complaint) against another, readily pardoning each other; even as the Lord has [freely] forgiven you, so must you also [forgive].
>
> *Colossians 3:13 AMPC*

You will also have people you pour your life into who will walk away. Remember the parable of the sower. Most don't make it to become multipliers. Even Jesus had one of his twelve not make it. Yes, it's heartbreaking when someone walks away, but let's not let it be because we started pulling back in our investment of them. Let's ask God to give us faith that He can radically change people's lives. Disciple making really isn't about us. Our part is being persistent and showing up. God does all the heavy lifting. Many people don't make it, but it is all worth it for the ones that do make it and become disciple makers themselves.

> I have no greater joy than this, to hear that my [spiritual] children are living their lives in the Truth.
>
> *3 John 1:4 AMPC*

Don't give up on people. Believe that God can do amazing things in and through their lives and you will be surprised by how some of them step up.

- *Feeling like you must give everyone the same amount of your time*

> And He appointed twelve to continue to be with Him, and that He might send them out to preach [as apostles or special messengers]
>
> *Mark 3:14 AMPC*

Jesus wasn't very fair in His investment in people He chose. All people are equally valuable, but not all people are equally strategic. We need to move with the movers. Some people don't really want more than a weekly meeting with you for discipleship, so don't waste your time chasing those people around. There may even come a point when you stop meeting with them and get them plugged into a community group or find someone else to invest in them. Find those you can really pour yourself into and help them as much as possible.

> Many a man proclaims his own loving-kindness and goodness, but a faithful man who can find?
>
> *Proverbs 20:6 AMPC*

If you find a faithful person you have found a rare specimen! Multiply your life into that person. Forget about being fair. Jesus wasn't. Jesus had the masses who followed Him, then He had seventy, then he had twelve, then three He brought to special occasions and one to whom He called His beloved. We would be wise to model our ministry strategies off of Jesus. Never apologize for investing more in faithful people than in others. Why? Because our goal is multiplication.

To request a complete catalog featuring books, DVDs, and CDs by Dr. John A. Tetsola, or to contact his for speaking engagements please write or call:

ECCLESIA WORD MINISTRIES INTERNATIONAL
P.O. BOX 743
BRONX, NEW YORK 10462

Phone: (718) 904-8530
Fax: (718) 904-8107

Please visit our website at www.ecclesiaword.org or you may send an email to reformers@msn.com.